50 Ultimate Corn Salad Recipes

(50 Ultimate Corn Salad Recipes - Volume 1)

Megan Murphy

Copyright: Published in the United States by Megan Murphy/ © MEGAN MURPHY

Published on December, 07 2020

All rights reserved. No part of this publication may be reproduced, stored in retrieval system, copied in any form or by any means, electronic, mechanical, photocopying, recording or otherwise transmitted without written permission from the publisher. Please do not participate in or encourage piracy of this material in any way. You must not circulate this book in any format. MEGAN MURPHY does not control or direct users' actions and is not responsible for the information or content shared, harm and/or actions of the book readers.

In accordance with the U.S. Copyright Act of 1976, the scanning, uploading and electronic sharing of any part of this book without the permission of the publisher constitute unlawful piracy and theft of the author's intellectual property. If you would like to use material from the book (other than just simply for reviewing the book), prior permission must be obtained by contacting the author at author@slushierecipes.com

Thank you for your support of the author's rights.

Content

50 AWESOME CORN SALAD RECIPES 4

1. "Maque Choux" Pasta Salad 4
2. Amagansett Corn Salad 4
3. Arugula And Grilled Corn Salad With Rosemary Vinaigrette 5
4. Black Bean & Corn Salad With Balsamic Vinegar Reduction 5
5. Black Bean Corn Salad 5
6. Black Bean And Roasted Corn Salad 6
7. Cheater's Tacos With Corn Salad 6
8. Colorful Fresh Corn Salad With Lime Vinaigrette 7
9. Corn Salad With Cilantro & Caramelized Onions 7
10. Corn Salad With Pedro Ximenez, Crispy Shallots, Radicchio And Pistachios 8
11. Corn Salad With Tomatoes, Avocado, Quinoa And Feta 8
12. Creamy Jalapeno Corn Salad 9
13. Crispy Salmon With Corn, Blackberry & Shishito Salad 9
14. Dilled, Crunchy Sweet Corn Salad With Buttermilk Dressing 10
15. Elotes Inspired Grilled Corn Salad 11
16. Fresh Tomato Soup With Grilled Corn Relish 11
17. Grilled Corn Salad 12
18. Grilled Corn Salad With Green Goddess Dressing 12
19. Grilled And Zesty Lime Corn Salad 13
20. Hatfield Corn Salad 13
21. Heirloom Tomato And Grilled Corn Salad 13
22. Homemade #ADOBO #seasoning Mix & Dry Rub 14
23. Kañiwa And Roasted Corn Salad 14
24. MEDITERRANEAN CORN SALAD 15
25. Mexican Corn Salad 15
26. Mexican Street Corn Salad 15
27. Minty Fregola & Grilled Corn Salad 16
28. Peppery, Tangy Corn Salad 16
29. Raw Corn Salad 17
30. Raw Corn Salad With Tomatoes, Feta, And Herbs 17
31. Raw Heirloom Tomato & Corn Salad 17
32. Refreshing Edamame And Corn Salad With Lime 18
33. Rhubarb Succotash 18
34. Roasted Mexican Street Corn Salad 19
35. Shrimp Boil Potato Salad 19
36. Shrimp And Corn Salad With Lime Dressing 20
37. Smokey Grilled Potato And Corn Salad 20
38. Spicy Corn Salad 21
39. Summer Corn Salad (inspired By Ina Garten's Confetti Corn Salad) 21
40. Summer Corn Salad With Toasted Grains 22
41. Summer Grilled Corn Salad 23
42. Summertime Fresh Corn Salad 23
43. THE BEST VEGAN CORN TACOS WITH BELL PEPPER AND CILANTRO 23
44. Thai Basil Corn Salad 24
45. Tomato And Grilled Corn Salad With Smoked Salt 24
46. Tuna And Corn Salad 25
47. Warm Red Cabbage And Corn Salad 25
48. Anatomy Of A Grilled Corn Salad 26
49. Cake 27
50. Quinoa And Corn Salad 27

INDEX 28
CONCLUSION 30

50 Awesome Corn Salad Recipes

***

1. "Maque Choux" Pasta Salad

Serving: Serves 4 | Prep: 0hours0mins | Cook: 0hours0mins | Ready in:

Ingredients

- 5 ears raw corn
- 1/2 pound andouille sausage
- 1 poblano pepper
- 1 cup dry orzo
- 2 medium plum tomatoes
- 2 large green onions
- 3 tablespoons extra virgin olive oil(and maybe a little more for finishing)
- 1 teaspoon of your favorite Creole/Cajun seasoning(I used Tony Chachere's original) and maybe a little more for finishing

Direction

- With a sharp knife, remove the kernels from the ears of corn. I do this in a large bowl so I don't have "flying" kernels. Set that bowl aside.
- Cut the andouille link lengthwise and then, if you like crosswise. On a grill or grill pan, grill the sausage and the poblano pepper until everything is lightly charred.
- Remove the seeds from the poblano and dice finely. Slice the grilled andouille into thin half-moons. Add both ingredients to the bowl of corn.
- Cook the orzo per package instructions. Drain and while still hot, stir it into the bowl of corn, andouille and pepper.
- Stir in the olive oil, sprinkle the Cajun/Creole seasoning over and stir again.
- Seed and core the tomatoes and cut into a small dice and then thinly slice the green onions. Stir them into the pasta salad. Cover and chill. When ready to serve, taste for seasoning and or extra olive oil.

2. Amagansett Corn Salad

Serving: Serves 4 | Prep: | Cook: |Ready in:

Ingredients

- 8 ears of white corn
- 2 quarts cherry tomatoes
- 3 tablespoons high-quality balsamic vinegar
- 1 medium red onion
- 1 quart sugar snap peas (optional)
- 1 handful roughly chopped basil or flat-leaf parsley (optional)
- Salt, preferably a large, coarse sea salt like Maldon.
- Pepper

Direction

- Strip raw corn from ears. Yep, raw. You can use a fancy corn stripper or just run your chef's knife down the side of each ear about 8 times.
- Slice all cherry tomatoes in half or quarters depending on your preference.
- Chop the red onion into a large dice.
- If using the sugar snap peas (they can be hard to find when the corn and tomatoes are available -- their seasons barely overlap, and even then you're likely getting corn and tomatoes from the south and sugar snaps from the North.) Anyway, if using them, cut in half or thirds to make more bite-sized. If you're not using them, and you want a little green for

visual appeal, some roughly chopped basil or flat-leaf parsley will do the trick.
- Toss all vegetables in a bowl, along with the vinegar, salt, and pepper.
- That's it. Enjoy!

3. Arugula And Grilled Corn Salad With Rosemary Vinaigrette

Serving: Serves 4-6 | Prep: | Cook: | Ready in:

Ingredients

- Arugula and Grilled Corn Salad
- 8-10 cups Baby arugula
- 1/2 cup Toasted walnuts
- 1/2 cup Crumbled goat cheese
- 1 cup Kernels from grilled corn
- Rosemary Vinaigrette
- 1-2 sprigs Rosemary
- 1/2 cup Olive oil
- 1/4 cup Champagne vinegar
- Pinch Salt
- Pinch Pepper

Direction

- Arugula and Grilled Corn Salad
- Assemble arugula, walnuts, goat cheese and corn on large serving platter. Drizzle with 2-4 T Rosemary Vinaigrette to taste.
- Rosemary Vinaigrette
- Make a rosemary infused oil by bruising rosemary with mallet and then heating it in pan with olive oil for about 5 minutes. Let cool. Remove rosemary from oil.
- Whisk rosemary oil, vinegar, salt and pepper to make vinaigrette.

4. Black Bean & Corn Salad With Balsamic Vinegar Reduction

Serving: Serves 4-6 | Prep: | Cook: | Ready in:

Ingredients

- Reduction
- 1/4 cup Balsamic Vinegar
- 1/4 cup Cider Vinegar
- 2 tablespoons Brown Sugar
- 1 1/2 teaspoons Fresh Lime Juice
- 1 Garlic Clove, pressed or minced
- 1/2 teaspoon Ground Cumin
- 1/4 teaspoon Salt
- Salad
- 1 cup Corn (off the cob. If using frozen, thaw first)
- 1 cup Red Bell Pepper, chopped
- 3/4 cup Chopped Sweet Onion
- 1/3 cup Cilantro, minced

Direction

- Add the Reduction ingredients to a small sauce pan.
- Bring ingredients to a boil, then simmer for 2 minutes.
- Put all Salad ingredients in a large bowl.
- Mix Reduced sauce in with the Salad ingredients.
- Place in fridge for a least an hour to cool (it's even better the next day).
- Serve with your favorite grilled meats & enjoy!

5. Black Bean Corn Salad

Serving: Serves 4-5 | Prep: | Cook: | Ready in:

Ingredients

- 1 can seasoned black beans, drained
- 3 ears of corn, steamed and kernels cut off of the cob
- 1 small onion, minced

- 2 garlic cloves, minced
- 1 jalapeno, minced
- juice from 1 lemon
- small handful fresh cilantro, chopped
- 1/8 to 1/4 cups olive oil
- salt and pepper to taste

Direction

- Basically, in a large bowl, combine black beans, corn, onion, garlic, cherry tomatoes, jalapeno, and lemon juice. Stir until well combined. Fold in cilantro.
- Drizzle with olive oil, to your own preference, and season with salt and pepper.

6. Black Bean And Roasted Corn Salad

Serving: Serves 8 to 10 as a side | Prep: | Cook: | Ready in:

Ingredients

- Brining and cooking the beans
- 1 pound dried black beans
- 3 tablespoons plus 1 teaspoon kosher salt
- 1 onion, halved
- Few sprigs thyme, optional
- 1 garlic clove, smashed
- Bean salad
- 4 cups cooked black beans
- 2 ears corn, kernels removed
- 2 red bell peppers, finely diced
- 1 to 2 jalapeños, diced (seeded if sensitive to heat)
- 1 medium red onion, finely diced
- 4 scallions, finely sliced, white and light green parts
- 1 small bunch cilantro, roughly chopped
- 1/4 to 1/2 cups extra-virgin olive oil, plus more for the corn
- 2 to 4 tablespoons white balsamic vinegar
- Kosher salt to taste

Direction

- Brine the beans: Place the beans in a large bowl with the 3 tablespoons of salt and water to cover by several inches. Let sit overnight or for 10 to 12 hours. Drain but do not rinse. Place beans in a large pot with the remaining teaspoon of salt, the onion, thyme, and garlic. Cover with water by several inches. Bring to a boil, then reduce heat so water is gently simmering. Simmer until beans are cooked through, 45 minutes to 1 hour. Let beans cool in their cooking liquid.
- Preheat the oven to 425° F. Place 4 cups of the cooked beans in a large strainer or colander. Do not rinse the beans. Let the beans drain as you prepare the salad.
- On a rimmed sheet pan, toss the corn kernels with 1 tablespoon olive oil. Season with salt and pepper to taste. Transfer pan to oven and roast for 10 minutes. Remove pan. Let kernels cool briefly.
- In a large mixing bowl, place the beans, corn, peppers, onion, scallions, and cilantro. Season with 1 teaspoon kosher salt. Dress with 1/4 cup olive oil and 2 tablespoons vinegar. Toss. Let stand 5 minutes, then toss again, taste, and adjust with more salt, oil and vinegar to taste. I add salt by the 1/2 teaspoon until it tastes right, and I keep a 2-to-1 oil-to-vinegar ratio for the most part—sometimes a splash more vinegar or a squeeze of lime at the end helps.

7. Cheater's Tacos With Corn Salad

Serving: Serves 4 | Prep: | Cook: | Ready in:

Ingredients

- Black bean and corn salsa
- 1 can black beans, drained and rinsed
- 2 ears corn, roasted and kernels cut off, or 1 can whole kernel corn
- 1 jar fire-roasted red peppers, diced

- 1 teaspoon smoked pimenton
- 1 teaspoon cumin
- 1/4 teaspoon cayenne pepper
- 4 tablespoons neutral flavored oil (I use canola)
- 2 tablespoons lime juice
- Fish tacos
- 1 recipe black bean and corn salsa
- 12 corn tortillas
- 12 2-oz fish sticks
- 1 avocado
- 1/4 teaspoon salt
- 1/4 teaspoon cayenne
- juice of one lime

Direction

- Combine beans, corn, seasonings, lime juice and salad oil. Set aside.
- Cook fish sticks according to package directions or your preference. Err on the side of extra crunchy coating.
- Blend avocado with lime juice, salt and cayenne.
- Assemble tacos. Spread guacamole in taco shell; top with fish stick, spoon black bean and corn salsa on top.
- Eat immediately, with prodigious quanties of Negro Modela Especial beer!

8. Colorful Fresh Corn Salad With Lime Vinaigrette

Serving: Serves 6-8 | Prep: | Cook: | Ready in:

Ingredients

- 5 ears of corn
- 1/2 red pepper diced
- 1/2 green pepper diced
- 1/2 yellow pepper diced
- 1/2 orange pepper diced
- 1/2 english cucumber unpeeled diced
- 1/2 red onion diced
- 4 scallions diced
- 2 tomatoes diced
- 1/4 cup parsley chopped
- 1/4 cup cilantro chopped
- 1 lime zested
- 1/4 cup freshly squeezed lime juice
- 1/4 cup rice vinegar
- 1/4 cup extra virgin olive oil
- 2 teaspoons cumin
- 2 teaspoons kosher salt

Direction

- Cook the corn either in boiling water for 2-3 minutes or you can microwave for 2-3 minutes. Slice the corn off the cob and place the kernels in a large mixing bowl. Add all the chopped vegetables, including the cilantro and parsley.
- In a small mixing bowl or food processor mix the lime zest, lime juice, olive oil, cumin and salt. Pour the dressing over the chopped vegetables and refrigerate till ready to serve.

9. Corn Salad With Cilantro & Caramelized Onions

Serving: Serves 6 | Prep: | Cook: | Ready in:

Ingredients

- 6 ears of fresh corn
- 6 slices pancetta
- 1 large red onion, peeled and diced
- 4 tablespoons olive oil
- 2 tablespoons balsamic vinegar
- 2 teaspoons sugar
- 1/4 cup finely chopped fresh cilantro
- salt and freshly ground pepper to taste

Direction

- Cook the corn on the cob in a large pot of boiling water for about 10 minutes. Drain hot water and plunge corn into a bowl of ice water

- to stop cooking. Drain corn and set aside to cool completely.
- Dice pancetta and cook in a heavy skillet over medium heat until brown and crispy. Use a slotted spoon to transfer pancetta to a plate lined with paper towels. Set aside.
- Pour off most of the pancetta fat from skillet, leaving a little goodness left in the pan for cooking your onions. Add oil, onions, vinegar, sugar, and dash of salt to pan, and cook over medium-low heat. Cook for about 20-25 minutes, stirring frequently until onions are caramelized and most of the liquid has evaporated. Remove pan from heat and set aside.
- Cut corn kernels off of the cobs and place in a large bowl. Add onion mixture and cilantro and stir to combine. Season to taste with salt and pepper and if it seems dry, add a little more olive oil.
- If you're making this ahead of time, cover and put it in the fridge. Take salad out about 3o minutes before serving to take chill off. Stir in crispy pancetta just before serving.

10. Corn Salad With Pedro Ximenez, Crispy Shallots, Radicchio And Pistachios

Serving: Serves 4-6 | Prep: | Cook: | Ready in:

Ingredients

- 8 shallots, medium size, sliced thin or early summer onions
- 2 tablespoons good olive oil, for cooking the shallots or onions
- 3 tablespoons Sherry Vinegar (SoTaroni Vinagre de vino Pedro ximenez gran reserva)
- 6 tablespoons good olive oil
- 6 corn ears, cooked and sliced off the cob
- 3/4 cups pistachios, roughly chopped and toasted
- 1 radicchio, large (or 2 medium), cut in half and sliced thin
- 1 pinch sea salt
- 1 pinch black pepper, fresh ground

Direction

- Heat olive oil to medium, add shallots or onions, cook until slightly crispy, but not burnt or dried out. Spoon into large salad bowl.
- Add sherry vinegar (SoTaroni Vinagre de vino Pedro Ximenez Gran Reserva), salt and pepper and whisk in remaining olive oil; add corn and mix well. Add additional salt and pepper if needed.
- Mix in the sliced radicchio and the pistachios and toss.
- Grilled shrimp can be added to turn this into a main course in the summer.

11. Corn Salad With Tomatoes, Avocado, Quinoa And Feta

Serving: Serves 4 as a side, 2 as a main course | Prep: | Cook: | Ready in:

Ingredients

- 1 ear of corn
- 2 medium-sized tomatoes, diced
- 2 avocado, diced
- 100 grams feta, crumbled
- 1/2 teaspoon paprika
- 1 teaspoon dried thyme
- 1 pinch of espelette pepper (or other mild pepper)
- 2 tablespoons lemon juice

Direction

- Bring a large pot of water to boil. Remove and discard the green outer husk and silky threads from the corn. Cook the ear of corn for 5

minutes then cool in a cold water bath. Remove the corn kernels and reserve in a bowl
- Rinse the quinoa under cold water. Put the quinoa and twice its volume in water in a pot and bring to boil. Reduce the heat and cook for 10 minutes with a lid. Let it stand for 5 minutes
- Make the dressing: mix the olive oil, lemon juice, pepper, cumin, paprika, thyme, salt and pepper
- Add the tomatoes, avocado, quinoa and corn. Stir well
- Top with the crumbled feta and serve

12. Creamy Jalapeno Corn Salad

Serving: Serves 8 | Prep: | Cook: | Ready in:

Ingredients

- Corn Salad
- 6 Ears of corn
- 1 chili pepper like a poblano, or whatever you prefer
- vegetable oil
- Creamy Jalapeno dressing
- 1 - 4.5 ounces can of green chiles
- 4 ounces sour cream
- 1/4 cup mayonnaise
- 1 bunch cilantro
- Juice of 1 lime
- 3 cloves of garlic, minced
- 1/3 jalapeno, minced
- 1.5 tablespoons water from a jar of pickled jalapenos

Direction

- Remove the corn from the cobs.
- Oil a grill or grill pan and grill the pepper until charred all over. Alternatively, you could also roast it in the oven until blistered. Let cool then peel off the skin and de-seed.
- Place all of the dressing ingredients in a food processor and process until smooth. This will make about a cup of dressing.
- Chop the pepper.
- Combine the corn and pepper with 1/2 cup + 1 tablespoon of the dressing.

13. Crispy Salmon With Corn, Blackberry & Shishito Salad

Serving: Serves 2 | Prep: 0hours25mins | Cook: 0hours25mins | Ready in:

Ingredients

- 2 ears corn, shucked
- 6 ounces blackberries
- Kosher salt, to taste
- 6 teaspoons canola oil, divided
- 4 ounces shishito peppers
- 2 (1/2-pound) salmon fillets
- Freshly ground black pepper, to taste
- 2 tablespoons extra-virgin olive oil
- 1 tablespoon freshly squeezed lime juice, plus more to taste
- 2 lime cheeks, for serving

Direction

- Take 1 ear of corn and use a very sharp knife to cut the kernels off the cob. Add those to a bowl. Halve the larger blackberries lengthwise, but leave the smaller ones as they are. Add all the blackberries to the bowl with the corn. Season with a pinch of salt and toss.
- Heat a large cast-iron over medium heat. While that heats up, de-kernel the remaining ear of corn. When the pan is hot, add 2 teaspoons canola oil. Swirl the oil around, then add the just-cut corn (not the corn with the blackberries! We want that to stay raw). Season with a pinch of salt, stir, then leave the corn alone to cook for about 6 minutes, stirring maybe once or twice, until it's golden-brown and starting to char. Push aside the corn-

blackberry mixture so half of the bowl is empty, then dump the crispy corn there to cool.

- With the pan still over medium heat, add another 2 teaspoons canola oil, then the shishitos and another pinch of salt. Cook in the same way—mostly leaving alone—for 6 minutes, until charred and deflated. Dump onto a cutting board to cool a bit and turn off the heat.
- Wipe out the skillet. Dry the salmon all over (this will encourage better browning), then season it generously with salt and black pepper. Turn the heat under the skillet on again, this time to medium-high. When the pan is hot, add the remaining 2 teaspoons canola oil. When the oil is shimmering, carefully add the salmon, skin side-down—it should loudly sizzle. Immediately lower the heat to medium-low and press down the salmon with a fish spatula, to prevent the skin from curling. Cook for 5 to 10 minutes, pressing down with the spatula occasionally, until the skin is deeply browned and crispy, and the flesh is nearly at the temperature you'd want to eat it at (I aim for 125°F for medium-rare). Flip the salmon and cook for another minute, then turn off the heat and remove it from the pan.
- While the salmon is cooking, chop the shishitos into smaller pieces (figure into thirds or fourths depending on the size of the pepper). Add these shishitos to the bowl with the corn and blackberries. Dress with the olive oil and lime juice. Toss and taste. Adjust with more olive oil, lime juice, and salt as needed.
- Serve the salmon with the salad on top or alongside, with a lime cheek to squeeze on top of the fish.

14. Dilled, Crunchy Sweet Corn Salad With Buttermilk Dressing

Serving: Serves 6 as a side dish | Prep: 0hours40mins | Cook: 0hours0mins | Ready in:

Ingredients

- For the salad:
- 1 clove shallot, halved lengthwise and thinly sliced
- 3 ears of fresh, uncooked corn, the kernels scraped from the cobs with a sharp knife (about 2 3/4 cup)
- 4 Persian cucumbers, quartered lengthwise and sliced crosswise into 1/2 inch dice
- 1 long red sweet pepper, seeded, ribs removed and diced
- 1 small handfull fresh dill (about 4 smallish sprigs), minced
- 1/4 cup minced fresh parsley
- 1 handful crumbled Feta cheese, rinsed, as a garnish
- For the dressing:
- 1/4 cup buttermilk
- 2/3 cup plain European style thin yogurt, stirred
- 1 tablespoon white-wine vinegar
- 3 tablespoons minced Vidalia or other sweet onion
- 1 small clove garlic, minced and mashed with a pinch of salt
- 1/4 cup extra-virgin olive oil
- salt and freshly ground pepper to taste.

Direction

- Salt the shallot slices in 1/2 t. salt and allow to sit about 20 minutes to draw out any harshness. Rinse well with water and pat dry with a paper towel. In a large bowl toss the corn kernels lightly to separate them, add the shallot and the remaining salad ingredients and toss again to combine.
- In a smaller bowl combine the buttermilk, vinegar, onion, yogurt, and garlic and whisk to combine. Add the oil in a slow stream,

whisking, until amalgamated. Season with freshly ground pepper and salt to taste.
- Serve the salad slightly chilled, garnished with the feta cheese. Pass the dressing separately.

15. Elotes Inspired Grilled Corn Salad

Serving: Serves 4 | Prep: | Cook: | Ready in:

Ingredients

- 3 Cobs of Corn
- 3 Green Onions
- 1 Avocado
- 1 Lime
- 1/4 cup Cilantro
- 1 tablespoon Mayonnaise
- 1 tablespoon Sour Cream
- 1/4 cup Cotija (feta works too)
- 1/4 teaspoon Chipotle powder

Direction

- Soak the corn in its husks for 30 minutes and then place on the BBQ for 15 minutes.
- Once the corn has steamed in its husks remove from the grill and discard husks.
- Slice the avocado in half and remove the stone.
- Place corn cobs, avocado and green onions on the grill to char.
- In a small bowl mix mayonnaise, sour cream, chipotle, and the juice and zest of half a lime.
- Remove corn from husks and place in a large bowl along with the chopped avocado and green onions.
- Chop the cilantro and crumble the cheese and add these with the dressing to the bowl.
- Toss the salad and season to taste.

16. Fresh Tomato Soup With Grilled Corn Relish

Serving: Serves 4 | Prep: 0hours20mins | Cook: 0hours38mins | Ready in:

Ingredients

- Tomato Soup
- 8 cups fresh tomatoes, chopped into 1 inch pieces
- 1 medium sweet onion, chopped into 8 pieces
- 4 garlic cloves, peeled
- 2 tablespoons olive oil
- 1/2 teaspoon salt
- 1/4 teaspoon black pepper
- 1/4 teaspoon dried oregano
- 1/2 teaspoon dried basil
- 2 cups vegetable stock
- 6 ounces tomato paste
- Grilled Corn Relish
- 2 ears of fresh corn, shucked and cleaned
- 1/4 medium red onion, chopped fine
- 1/2 jalapeño
- 1/4 teaspoon cumin
- 1 tablespoon fresh basil, chopped fine
- 1 tablespoon olive oil
- Pinch of salt and sugar to taste

Direction

- Pre-heat oven to 450°
- Wash tomatoes (you can use large tomato, cherry, roma or a mixture). Chop into 1 inch pieces.
- Place tomatoes, onion, garlic cloves, olive oil, salt, pepper, oregano and basil on a large backing sheet and mix with hands to combine.
- Bake for 30 minutes, stirring halfway through baking.
- In the meantime, add vegetable stock and tomato paste to a large stockpot and heat over medium heat. Whisk to combine.
- Once the tomato mixture is finished roasting, add to the stockpot with the vegetable broth and tomato paste and remove from heat.

- Using an immersion blender, blend until soup is silky smooth. Keep warm.
- To make the corn relish, pre-heat grill to high. Place corn and jalapeño on grill. Turn once a minute for about 8 minutes, until cooked through and full of beautiful grill marks. Remove from grill. Using tongs or heat proof gloves, slice corn kernels off the cob into a medium bowl. Cut jalapeño in half and remove all of the seed and dice small. Add remaining ingredients to bowl and mix.
- To serve, divide soup into 4 bowls and top with corn relish.

17. Grilled Corn Salad

Serving: Serves 4 | Prep: | Cook: | Ready in:

Ingredients

- 4 ears white corn
- drizzle olive oil
- 1 pint cherry tomatoes
- 1/4 of a red onion, diced
- cilantro, handful, minced
- 1 avocado, medium dice
- 1 lemon, juiced
- drizzle of high quality olive oil
- 2 teaspoons cumin seeds, lightly toasted
- kosher salt, to taste

Direction

- Heat your BBQ grill. Lightly coat the corn with some olive oil, grill, just until there are slight grill marks. Let cool.
- While the corn is grilling, let the onion sit in an icy bowl of water, to remove the bitterness, for at least 30 minutes; drain.
- Toss cherry tomatoes into a serving bowl. I used really tiny ones, if you cannot find really tiny ones, cut them in half.
- Add the onion and the cilantro.
- Carefully, slice the corn kernels off of the ears of corn, add to the bowl.
- In a small jar or bowl, mix olive oil, lemon juice and cumin. Drizzle over the corn mixture. Add the avocado.
- Season with salt. Toss.
- Serve. Eat.

18. Grilled Corn Salad With Green Goddess Dressing

Serving: Serves a crowd | Prep: | Cook: | Ready in:

Ingredients

- 12 ears of corn
- Cherry Tomatoes (halved)
- 1 tablespoon Dijon Musard
- 1 teaspoon Honey
- 1/4 cup Rice Wine Vinegar
- 1/2 cup Exta Virgin Olive Oil
- 1 bunch Green Onion, green part only
- salt and pepper to taste

Direction

- Remove the husk and the silk from the corn. Line your grill with Aluminum Foil. Grill your corn on a medium low flame turning occasionally until grill marks appear. Approximately 20 mins.
- While corn is grilling, start the dressing. In a blender or food processor add the Dijon Mustard, Honey, Rice Wine Vinegar. Chop the Green Onion and add into the mixture. While mixing slowly drizzle in the Extra Virgin Olive Oil. Mix until all ingredients are incorporated and is smooth like a dressing. Salt and Pepper to taste.
- When corn is cool enough to handle, with a sharp knife cut the kernels off the cob. Drizzle corn with the dressing and top with Cherry Tomatoes. ENJOY!

19. Grilled And Zesty Lime Corn Salad

Serving: Serves 6 | Prep: | Cook: | Ready in:

Ingredients

- 4 Corn Cobs
- 1 Pasilla Pepper
- 1 Avocado
- 2 sprigs Green Onion
- 1 cup Heirloom Tomato
- 1 Lime
- 1 teaspoon Sea Salt
- 1 teaspoon Fresh Ground Black Pepper
- 2 tablespoons Olive Oil

Direction

- Put the husked corn cobs, green onion, and pepper on the outer edges of a hot grill. (Or over the flame on your stove)
- Thoroughly blacken the edges, turning as they cook. They shouldn't be totally blackened, but definitely give them a good char.
- Let them cool to the touch, then cut the kernels of the cobs, roughly chop the pepper, and the green onions (include the bulbs, discard the roots).
- Add these to a medium sized bowl. Chop the tomato and add that too.
- Zest and juice the lime adding them to the mix. Add salt, pepper, olive oil.
- Mix. Finally chop the avocado and add that as well, then mix lightly retaining the structure of your avocado.

20. Hatfield Corn Salad

Serving: Serves 4 | Prep: | Cook: | Ready in:

Ingredients

- 6 ears of corn
- 1 red onion
- 1/2 pint heirloom cherry tomatoes
- 1/2 cup fresh basil
- 3 tablespoons olive oil
- 3 tablespoons red wine vinegar
- corn milk
- salt and pepper to taste

Direction

- Boil corn for 2 minutes, turning halfway through. Cool in ice bath.
- Cut corn off cob. Using the back of a chef's knife, run down the cobs to get the corn milk.
- Quarter the tomatoes, shred the basil, and finely dice the red onion.
- Mix ingredients in bowl, refrigerate and serve.

21. Heirloom Tomato And Grilled Corn Salad

Serving: Serves 2 quarts | Prep: 0hours30mins | Cook: 0hours10mins | Ready in:

Ingredients

- 6 ears corn, husked
- 4 cups tomatoes, chopped coarsely (you can also use cherry tomatoes and halve or quarter them)
- 1/2 cup Vidalia onion, diced
- 1/2 cup Parsley (flat leafed or curly) chopped
- 1/2 jalapeno pepper, minced
- 1/2 cup Good olive oil
- juice of one lime
- Kosher or sea salt, to taste
- Ground black pepper, to taste

Direction

- Rub the husked corn with a little olive oil, salt, and pepper. Place on outdoor grill and turn until some of the kernels are a little blackened.
- With a sharp knife, remove the kernels from the cobs. Be sure to then use the dull side of

the knife blade to scrape off the "milk". Place in a medium sized bowl.
- Put all the rest of the chopped and minced ingredients in the bowl with the corn.
- Make a dressing with the olive oil and lime juice; season to taste with salt and pepper. Pour into the bowl with all the ingredients, and mix thoroughly.

22. Homemade #ADOBO #seasoning Mix & Dry Rub

Serving: Makes 1 batch lasting 4-6 weeks, if you cook everyday. | Prep: 0hours20mins | Cook: 0hours0mins | Ready in:

Ingredients

- 1 cup ground Cumin (Geera)
- 1 cup Garlic Powder
- 1 cup onion Powder
- 1 cup sea salt-Finely ground
- 1/2 cup thyme
- 1/2 cup Cayenne pepper (Chilli Powder) =OPTIONAL
- 1 cup Black Pepper
- 1/2 cup oregano

Direction

- Add all ingredients into one container (glass or plastic) with wide mouth, thoroughly mix it all together. Remove about 1 cup of the mix to your daily use jar and place the large container in a paper bag and just leave it on your pantry shelf.
- Use about 1 tablespoon per pound of vegetables or meat or fish. You may also use it as a dry rub to Bar-B-Que, smoke, braise or oven roast meats. You may also sprinkle this Adobo on vegetables before grilling.

23. Kañiwa And Roasted Corn Salad

Serving: Serves 4 | Prep: | Cook: | Ready in:

Ingredients

- 1 cup kañiwa, rinsed in a fine sieve
- 2 cups water
- 2 cups roasted corn, frozen*
- 3 jarred, roasted peppers, rinsed and chopped
- 1/2 Vidalia onion, chopped
- 1 cup packed, cilantro leaves, rinsed and chopped
- 1 15 oz. can small white beans, drained and rinsed
- 2 limes, juiced
- 1/2 teaspoon cumin powder
- 2 teaspoons olive oil [optional]

Direction

- It is recommended to toast the kañiwa before cooking. Rinse and then place in a dry skillet. Stir over high heat until water boils off. Once dry, toast kañiwa for 1 minute, constantly moving it around the pan.
- Place in rice cooker with 2 cups of water and turn on. It took less than 15 minutes for perfect texture. You could follow package directions and prepare it stove top as well.
- In a large bowl, mix corn, peppers, onion, cilantro, and beans. Whisk lime juice with cumin and olive oil [add oil if desired, but not necessary] and add to vegetables.
- * Whole Foods and Trader Joe's sell frozen organic roasted corn, but you could also throw some leftover cobs on the grill for a few minutes and remove kernels.
- Nutrition facts per serving: Calories, 312; Total fat, 3g; Total Carbohydrate, 62g; Fiber, 10g; Protein, 14g; Iron, 25% DV; Vit C, 46% DV; Vit A, 12% DV

24. MEDITERRANEAN CORN SALAD

Serving: Serves 10-12 | Prep: | Cook: | Ready in:

Ingredients

- 4 cups Sweet Corn Nibs (off the cob)
- 2 cups Cucumber diced
- 2 cups Garbanzo Beans
- 1.5 cups Feta Cheese
- 1 cup Walnuts
- 1 garlic clove
- 3 tablespoons extra virgin olive oil
- 1/4 cup Oregano
- 1/4 cup Lemon Juice
- 1 pinch Pepper & Salt

Direction

- Heat a cast iron pan to high. Cook corn in dry pan till browned about 3 minutes.
- Transfer to a large bowl with cucumber, chickpeas, and walnuts.
- Mix in lemon juice, oregano, olive oil, and garlic & feta
- Serve immediately or chill until ready to serve.

25. Mexican Corn Salad

Serving: Serves 6 - 8, easily doubled or trippled | Prep: | Cook: | Ready in:

Ingredients

- 1/4 cup mayonnaise (or more to taste)
- juice of 2 limes
- 1 teaspoon mild chili powder
- 1/2 teaspoon ground cumin
- 8 ears fresh corn, shucked and silks removed
- 1 cup crumbled cotija cheese
- salt to taste

Direction

- In a small bowl, mix together the mayonnaise, juice of one lime, the chili powder and the ground cumin. Blend well and set aside.
- Cook the corn on the cob. You can bring a large pot of water to the boil, drop in the cobs and bring the water back to the boil. Remove the pot from the heat, cover it and let the cobs cook for five minutes. If you've got the grill going, you can then place the cobs on the grill to get a nice char on the kernels, but it's fine if you don't grill.
- When cool enough to handle, cut the kernels from the cobs using a sharp knife. Place the corn in a large bowl and squeeze over the juice of one lime.
- Toss the kernels around to absorb the lime juice. Add the cotija cheese and toss to combine. Stir in the mayonnaise dressing to coat all the corn kernels.
- Add salt to taste and mix well. This salad will keep covered in the fridge for 24 hours.

26. Mexican Street Corn Salad

Serving: Serves 4 | Prep: | Cook: | Ready in:

Ingredients

- 6 ears of corn, husks and silks removed
- Olive oil cooking spray
- Salt and pepper
- 1/4 cup mayonnaise
- 1/4 cup sour cream
- Zest and juice of a lime
- 1 teaspoon ancho chili powder
- 1/4 teaspoon onion powder
- 1/4 cup cilantro leaves, plus more for garnish
- 6 ounces cotija cheese, crumbled

Direction

- Preheat oven to broil or prepare grill at high heat. Spray each corn cob with cooking spray and season with salt and pepper. Broil or grill the corn, turning every few minutes to char

- the kernels. Remove and cool. Cut the corn from the cob into a large mixing bowl.
- In a small bowl, whisk together mayonnaise, sour cream, 1/2 teaspoon salt, lime juice and zest, ancho and onion powders. Pour the dressing over the corn and toss to coat. Stir in the chopped cilantro and place the corn salad onto a large serving platter.
- Top the corn salad with the cheese and serve with some sprigs of cilantro and lime wedges alongside.

27. Minty Fregola & Grilled Corn Salad

Serving: Serves 4-5 | Prep: | Cook: |Ready in:

Ingredients

- Fregola salad
- 1/2 cup Fregola or Israeli cous cous
- 2 ears of corn removed from the cob
- 1/2 hot house cucumber finely diced
- 1 roma tomato deseeded & finely chopped
- 1 thai chilli deseeded & finely minced
- 25-30 fresh mint leaves
- 1 tablespoon Canola or olive oil
- 1 handful of toasted chopped walnuts or pecans
- Minty chat masala dressing
- 1/4 cup mint flavored extra virgin Olive oil (see last step)
- 2 tablespoons Chat masala spice blend (available at any Indian grocery
- Juice of 1 lime
- 1 tablespoon Honey

Direction

- Toast the Fregola until it turns a pale brown color, add to 2 cups of boiling water. Cover & cook for about 5-6 minutes until the Fregola turns soft. Strain out any excess water and rinse thoroughly with cold water to stop the cooking process.
- Heat a cast iron skillet till very hot and drizzle the olive oil, when it just begins to smoke, add the corn kernels & spread into a single layer allow to roast on the pan for about 5 minutes on medium high until the kernel begins to develop tiny brown spots. Shake the pan & continue roasting the corn for 2 minutes more. Switch off the heat and allow the corn to brown lightly in the pan's residual heat. Transfer to a mixing bowl along with the fregola.
- Roll the mint leaves and cut them very fine in a chiffonade. Chop the chiffonaded leaves further using a sharp knife to obtain tiny shreds of mint. Add this to the mixing bowl along with the diced tomato, cucumber, walnut and Thai chili.
- In a smaller bowl combine the lime juice, honey and chat masala & whisk to dissolve the honey. Add the mint flavored olive oil and whisk into a dressing. Pour over the corn & Fregola salad and lightly toss to combine. Place in refrigerator to chill and allow for the flavors to blend. Spoon into bowls and serve with a side of pita chips.

28. Peppery, Tangy Corn Salad

Serving: Serves 2-3 | Prep: | Cook: |Ready in:

Ingredients

- 2 ears yellow corn
- 2.5 c arugula
- 1/4 c red onion, diced
- 1/4 c ricotta salata, grated
- 4 tbsp extra virgin olive oil
- 2 tbsp fresh squeezed lemon juice
- 4-5 basil leaves, chopped
- fresh ground pepper to taste
- pinch of salt

Direction

- Boil corn ears for 3 minutes, then submerge in an ice bath. Once cooled, shave the corn and put aside. In a large salad bowl, add the arugula and red onion. Add the ricotta, olive oil, lemon juice, basil, fresh ground pepper, and salt. Now add the corn. (You may be wondering why the corn isn't tossed in first with the arugula. Good question! You don't want to welt the arugula by having a few warm corn kernels.
- Serve at room temperature.

29. Raw Corn Salad

Serving: Serves 4 | Prep: | Cook: | Ready in:

Ingredients

- 6 Ears of fresh corn
- 1 Avocado, chopped
- 2-3 tablespoons Chopped cilantro
- 1/2-1 Lime
- 1/2 Jalapeño minced
- Salt
- Pepper

Direction

- Remove corn kernels from ears and place in medium bowl
- Add rest of ingredients. Toss to combine. Add salt and pepper to taste

30. Raw Corn Salad With Tomatoes, Feta, And Herbs

Serving: Serves 4 | Prep: 0hours30mins | Cook: 0hours0mins | Ready in:

Ingredients

- 4 ears corns, shucked
- 1 pint cherry tomatoes, halved
- 4 ounces feta, crumbled (I prefer in-brine varieties)
- 1 cup finely chopped basil
- 1/4 cup finely chopped mint
- 16 ounces cooked beans, such as chickpeas, black beans, or white beans, optional, see notes above
- kosher salt and pepper to taste
- 4 to 6 tablespoons extra virgin olive oil
- 1 lime, halved

Direction

- Line a shallow bowl or plate with a kitchen towel. Use one hand to hold an ear of corn in place upright atop the kitchen towel. With your other hand, use a knife to cut off two to three rows of kernels at a time by sliding the knife down the cob. Get as close to the cob as you can. Transfer corn to a bowl with the tomatoes, feta, and herbs. If using the chickpeas or beans, add them to the bowl as well.
- Add 1/2 teaspoon kosher salt and pepper to taste. Add 4 tablespoons oil and the juice of half a lime. Toss and taste. Add another 1/2 teaspoon salt if necessary and more pepper to taste. If it needs more acidity, squeeze in the remaining lime. If it needs more dressing, drizzle in the remaining 2 tablespoons oil. Toss. Serve immediately.

31. Raw Heirloom Tomato & Corn Salad

Serving: Serves 8-12 | Prep: | Cook: | Ready in:

Ingredients

- 2 Heirloom Tomatoes
- 1 Zucchini
- 1 Cucumber
- 1 Red Onion
- 1 Bell Pepper
- 1/8 cup Organic Cold Pressed Olive Oil

- 1/4 cup Organic White Wine Vinegar
- 1/4 teaspoon Garlic Powder
- 1/2 teaspoon Organic Oregano
- 1/2 teaspoon Organic Basil
- 1/2 teaspoon Organic Italian Seasoning
- 8 pieces Corn

Direction

- Chop Heirloom Tomatoes and Zucchini into 1-2" cubes
- Peel and Chop Cucumber into 1-2" cubes
- Peel and dice Red Onion
- Seed and dice Bell Pepper
- Husk, wash and cut kernels from corn (corn can be completely raw or you can blanch for 30-60 seconds by placing in boiling water one ear at a time prior to removing kernels)
- Place all ingredients in a bowl and drizzle with olive oil, stir to mix in oil
- Crush herbs in hand or use mortar and pestle to release flavors and oils
- Add crushed herbs and garlic powder to wine vinegar and mix
- Drizzle vinegar into bowl of other ingredients and mix
- Cover and place into refrigerator for a minimum of 1 hour, 8 hours or overnight is better

32. Refreshing Edamame And Corn Salad With Lime

Serving: Serves 1 3/4 cups | Prep: | Cook: | Ready in:

Ingredients

- 1/2 cup edamame beans, shelled
- 1 cup fresh corn cut from the cob, uncooked
- 1/2 cup red onion, finely chopped
- 1/2 red pepper, finely chopped
- 1 small plum or other meaty tomato, chopped
- 3/4 of a lime, juiced (or to taste)
- 5-6 small basil leaves, chopped
- 5-6 small mint leaves, chopped
- salt and pepper to taste

Direction

- Toss everything together and put in a container for lunch in the morning. By lunch, all the flavors will have come together beautifully and you've got a fabulous, healthy meal or side dish.
- Note: if you're making it to eat right away, let the mixture sit in a bowl for at least 30 minutes to allow the flavors to mingle.

33. Rhubarb Succotash

Serving: Serves 4-6 | Prep: 0hours10mins | Cook: 0hours15mins | Ready in:

Ingredients

- 2 ears of corn
- 4 stalks of rhubarb
- 2 cups cooked lima beans
- 1 small sweet onion
- 1 big ripe tomato
- Bunch of fresh parsley
- 2-3 tablespoons red wine vinegar
- olive oil
- Splash water

Direction

- Chop the onion into small pieces then chop the rhubarb into smallish chunks. Toss the rhubarb and onion into a skillet with just a tiny bit of olive oil and a splash of water. Place on the stove on medium heat and cook until the onion and rhubarb are slightly tender, but not falling apart soft. If you need to, add a bit more water to the skillet to keep the stuff from browning or burning.
- While the rhubarb is cooking, remove the corn from the cob and chop up the tomato into small chunks. Toss the corn, the tomato, the cooked lima beans (drained) into the skillet

with the rhubarb and onion. Pour in about 2-3 tablespoons of vinegar and season with salt and pepper. Mix and cook for another few minutes just until the corn get slightly cooked and all the flavors have had a few minutes to meld.

- Remove from heat and dump into a bowl. Chop up a handful of fresh parsley and sprinkle all over. Serve right away warm or stick in the fridge and serve cold later.

34. Roasted Mexican Street Corn Salad

Serving: Serves 6 as a side dish | Prep: | Cook: |Ready in:

Ingredients

- 6 ears of sweet corn, silks and husks removed
- Nonstick cooking spray
- 4 ounces diced green chiles
- 2 small garlic cloves, minced
- 1/2 small red onion, finely chopped (about 1/2 cup)
- 3/4 cup crumbled cotija or feta cheese, divided
- 1/4 cup coarsely chopped fresh cilantro
- 3 tablespoons fresh lime juice
- 2 tablespoons mayonnaise
- 2 tablespoons sour cream
- 1/2 teaspoon chili powder
- 1/8 teaspoon cayenne pepper (or 1/4 teaspoon if you'd like it more spicy)
- 1/4 teaspoon kosher salt

Direction

- Preheat oven to 375°. Cut corn kernels from cobs. Spray rimmed baking pan with nonstick spray. Spread corn in single layer on prepared pan. Roast 30 to 40 minutes or until golden brown, stirring twice.
- Meanwhile, in large bowl, stir together chiles, garlic, onion, 1/2 cup cheese, cilantro, lime juice, mayonnaise, sour cream, chili powder, cayenne and salt.
- Let corn cool slightly, then toss with mayonnaise mixture until well combined. Serve sprinkled with remaining 1/4 cup cheese.

35. Shrimp Boil Potato Salad

Serving: Serves 8 | Prep: 0hours15mins | Cook: 0hours25mins |Ready in:

Ingredients

- 3 pounds baby red potatoes, rinsed
- 4 ears corn, husks and silks removed
- 1 pound shrimp, peeled, deveined and tails removed
- 1/2 cup olive oil
- 1/4 cup plus 2 tablespoons lemon juice
- 3 tablespoons Old Bay Seasoning
- 3 tablespoons kosher salt, divided
- 2 teaspoons sugar
- 1/4 cup chopped chives, for serving

Direction

- Fill a large pot with water and bring to a boil. Once boiling, add two tablespoons of salt. Add the potatoes and cook until easily pierced with a knife, about 20 minutes. Using a spider or a slotted spoon, remove the potatoes to a bowl to cool.
- Return the pot of water to a boil and drop the whole cobs into the water. Blanch for 1 minute. Remove the corn and let cool. Bring water back to a boil. Add in the shrimp and immediately turn off the heat and remove the pot from the burner. Let poach in the hot water for 1 minute before removing to an ice bath. While everything cools make the dressing.
- In a large bowl, whisk together olive oil, lemon juice, Old Bay Seasoning, the remaining tablespoons of salt and sugar. Set aside.

- Once cool to the touch, slice each potato into four round slices and add to the bowl with the dressing. Cut the corn from the cob and add it to the bowl with the potatoes. Remove the shrimp from the ice bath, pat dry and add to the bowl as well. Toss until all the ingredients are well coated.
- Let chill in the fridge for at least 2 hours before serving. To serve, garnish with chives. This dish can be made up to two days in advance.

36. Shrimp And Corn Salad With Lime Dressing

Serving: Serves 2-3 | Prep: | Cook: | Ready in:

Ingredients

- For the shrimp
- 1/2 pound shrimp, peeled and deveined
- 2 tablespoons olive oil
- pinch salt
- pinch pepper
- 1/2 teaspoon paprika
- For the Salad
- 1 jalapeno, stem and seed removed, finely diced
- 1 ear of corn
- 2 tablespoons chives, finely chopped
- 1 tablespoon basil, chiffonade
- 1 lime, zested and juiced
- 1 teaspoon salt
- 1/4 teaspoon pepper
- 3-4 tablespoons olive oil
- 1 avocado, cut into chunks

Direction

- Toss shrimp in a bowl with the olive oil, a sprinkle of salt and pepper and ½ tsp. paprika. Let sit in the refrigerator for 30 minutes to an hour.
- Preheat your grill, grill pan or skillet.
- While your grill is preheating, combine the jalapeno, chives, basil, lime zest and juice, salt, pepper, olive oil and avocado in a bowl. Mix together. Set aside.
- Once your grill is preheated, grill your corn. Once it is almost done, 5-6 minutes, add the shrimp to the grill and cook 2-3 minutes per side or until pink and cooked through.
- Remove the shrimp and corn and let cool slightly. Remove the kernels from the cooled cob and place in the avocado and jalapeno bowl. Once the shrimp are cool enough to handle, chop up into ½ inch pieces. Add to bowl.
- Toss to combine and serve with butter lettuce as a salad or with chips.

37. Smokey Grilled Potato And Corn Salad

Serving: Serves 4-6 | Prep: | Cook: | Ready in:

Ingredients

- 2 pounds small red potatoes, scrubbed
- 4 scallions, trimmed
- 3 ears of corn, husked and silks removed
- 2 cloves of garlic - not peeled - skewered on a wooden stick
- 2-3 tablespoons olive oil
- 3/4 cup mayonnaise
- 1 - 2 teaspoons smoked paprika
- 1/2 teaspoon cumin
- 3 tablespoons Champagne vinegar
- 1 teaspoon lemon zest
- 1 bunch watercress, chopped

Direction

- To pre-cook the potatoes, place them whole in a stock pot of boiling salted water and cook for 15 - 20 minutes until they are just tender (this will depend greatly on the size of your potatoes). Drain and cool slightly so you can handle them. Cut in half or in quarters - depending on the size of your potatoes (but

big enough that they can sit on your grill grates and not fall through).
- Light your grill to medium high. Brush your potatoes, corn, scallions, and garlic with olive oil and season with salt and pepper. Grill the potatoes until they have nice grill marks - but they should be cooked through in step one.
- Grill the corn about 5 minutes - until it is nicely browned and charred in some spots. Grill the scallions about 2 minutes per side - until browned. Cook the garlic skewers on a cooler area of the grill, turning frequently, until the clove is softened but does not burn. (Depending on the size of the clove - 8-10 minutes).
- Place the potatoes in a bowl. Cut the corn off the cob and chop the scallions and place them in the bowl with the potatoes.
- Make the dressing: Peel and crush the garlic into a paste. Mix it with the mayo, (1-2 teaspoons - see headnote) smoked paprika, cumin, champagne vinegar, and lemon zest. Season with salt and pepper.
- Add the watercress to the potato mixture and pour the dressing over (see headnote - first start with half and add more to reach your desired creaminess) and fold in gently. Taste for seasoning. Can be served slightly warm, at room temp, or chilled.

38. Spicy Corn Salad

Serving: Serves 2 | Prep: | Cook: | Ready in:

Ingredients

- Corn
- 2 cups corn
- 2 red chilis, thinly sliced
- 1 tablespoon garlic, minced
- 1 teaspoon ginger, minced
- 2 teaspoons green onion, thinly sliced
- 5 basil leaves, in chiffonade
- 3 sprigs cilantro, chopped
- salt & pepper

- Sesame Chili Drizzle
- 1 teaspoon chili garlic sauce
- 1/2 teaspoon toasted sesame oil
- 1 tablespoon rice vinegar
- 1/2 teaspoon mirin

Direction

- Cook garlic, ginger, chilis and green onion in a tablespoon of oil until just starting to brown. Add corn and cook a few minutes more. If your corn is not as fabulously sweet as it should be you can add a pinch of sugar. Season with salt and pepper and stir in cilantro and basil.
- Mix all drizzle ingredients and toss into corn mixture. Enjoy room temperature.

39. Summer Corn Salad (inspired By Ina Garten's Confetti Corn Salad)

Serving: Serves 5-6 | Prep: | Cook: | Ready in:

Ingredients

- 1/2 cup chopped sweet onion
- 1 cup diced orange or red bell pepper
- 2 tablespoons unsalted butter
- 4 cups frozen corn (or 5 ears fresh corn)
- 2 tablespoons olive oil
- 1 1/2 teaspoons salt
- 1 teaspoon black pepper
- 2 tablespoons fresh basil

Direction

- In a large skillet, heat olive oil over medium heat. Add the onion and sauté for minutes, until soft and translucent. Add bell pepper and sauté for another 2-3 minutes.
- Add butter to the pan and allow to melt. Add the corn and cook for about 5 minutes.
- Turn off heat. Add salt, pepper and basil.
- Serve hot.

40. Summer Corn Salad With Toasted Grains

Serving: Serves 6 as a side | Prep: | Cook: | Ready in:

Ingredients

- 4 ears corn, shucked
- about 3/4 cups 2% Milk
- 3 strips of bacon, finely chopped
- 1/2 cup sweet onion, finely chopped
- 3 cloves garlic, peeled and smashed with the flat side of a large knife
- 2 tablespoons jalapeño, minced (with seeds and membranes -- you want a little heat)
- Pinch of salt
- 1 teaspoon maple syrup
- 1 cup quinoa, rinsed and drained
- 3/4 cup basmati rice
- 1 3/4 cups plus 2 tablespoons water
- 3 ounces Cotija cheese, crumbled
- 3 tablespoons finely snipped garlic chives
- 1/3 cup snipped cilantro
- Freshly ground black pepper

Direction

- Prep your corn the safe by placing one ear horizontally on a cutting board or the work surface in front of you. Hold one edge of the corn while slicing the kernels off the opposite side with a sharp knife. Rotate cob so that the flat, cut side is now sitting firmly on your work surface and repeat until you have cut around the entire ear. Repeat with remaining ears of corn. You should have between 2 to 3 cups of kernels (depending on the size of your ears). Place in a bowl and set aside.
- Milk your cobs one at a time by standing upright (trimming the end to make it sit flat if necessary) in a pie plate and, carefully work downwards, scraping the cob with the backside of your knife. Continue on all sides of the cob. Repeat with remaining cobs. Transfer mixture to a two cup or quart Pyrex measure -- you should have about 3/4 cup corn milk and pulp. Add enough dairy milk so that entire mixture measures 1 1/2 cups. Set aside.
- In a Dutch oven, cook bacon over medium heat until it's crispy and the fat has rendered. Using a slotted utensil, transfer bacon pieces to a small bowl and set aside.
- Add onion, flattened garlic, corn kernels, and jalapeño to bacon drippings. Add a pinch of salt and maple syrup. Cook for 5 minutes, stirring to ensure nothing burns. Transfer corn mixture to a bowl and set aside to cool.
- Return Dutch oven to heat and immediately add quinoa and basmati to begin toasting, stirring constantly to prevent burning. Toast until grains are fragrant and golden brown, about 6 minutes. Carefully add water (grains will sizzle and spit) turning heat down if necessary. Add reserved corn milk-dairy milk mixture from Pyrex. Bring mixture to a boil, cover, and reduce heat to low to simmer. Cook for 20 minutes, until liquid is completely absorbed and grains are tender.
- Gently fluff grains with a fork and transfer to a large serving bowl to cool. Help grains cool by pulling from the bottom of the bowl with a spatula, essentially folding from the bottom up.
- Once the grains have cooled a bit, fold in crispy bacon pieces and any oil that accumulated in the bowl. Continue to build the salad by thoroughly folding in the corn-onion-jalapeño mixture, then half of the Cotija cheese, half of the chives, and half of the cilantro. Your ingredients should be evenly distributed.
- Finish salad by topping with remaining cheese, chives, cilantro, and a few grinds of black pepper. Serve immediately or at room temperature. Enjoy!

41. Summer Grilled Corn Salad

Serving: Makes 2 cups | Prep: | Cook: |Ready in:

Ingredients

- 2 Large ears of grilled corn, kernels removed
- 1 Large jalapeno, gilled, skin removed and diced
- 1/2 cup Red onion, finely diced
- 1/2 Avocado, diced
- 1/2 cup Cherry tomatoes, quartered
- 1/4 cup Cilantro, roughly chopped
- 1 teaspoon Lime zest
- Juice of 2 limes
- 1 tablespoon olive oil
- Salt and pepper to taste

Direction

- In a bowl mix corn kernels, jalapeno, onion, avocado, cherry tomatoes, cilantro, lime zest lime juice, olive oil. Season with salt and pepper. Serve!!

42. Summertime Fresh Corn Salad

Serving: Serves 4-6 | Prep: | Cook: |Ready in:

Ingredients

- 2 fresh ears corn, shucked
- 1 cup fresh baby carrots
- 1/2 cup chopped bell pepper
- 1 fresh jalapeno, minced
- 1/2 cup pitted black olives, chopped
- 3/4 cup sliced scallions
- 1/2 cup chopped fresh tomato
- 1/2 cup crumbled cotija or feta cheese
- 2 tablespoons chopped fresh cilantro
- 1/2 teaspoon dried oregano
- salt to taste
- black pepper to taste
- 1/8 tablespoon garlic powder
- 2 tablespoons extra virgin olive oil
- 1 tablespoon white balsamic vinegar

Direction

- Par-cook corn and carrots in boiling salted water for 4 minutes, then drain.
- Cut corn from cobs and chop carrots.
- Combine all ingredients (discard cobs) for salad and refrigerate several hours before serving.

43. THE BEST VEGAN CORN TACOS WITH BELL PEPPER AND CILANTRO

Serving: Serves 5 tacos | Prep: 0hours15mins | Cook: 0hours40mins |Ready in:

Ingredients

- 1 cup corn flour
- 1 tablespoon tomato paste
- 3 bell peppers
- 2 onions
- 1 large clove of garlic
- 1 zucchini
- 1/4 tablespoon smoked paprika powder
- 2 pinches cinnamon
- 1/2 bunch fresh cilantro
- 2-3 tablespoons vegetable oil for sautéeing
- salt, pepper to taste

Direction

- Follow the instructions on the package of your corn flour and prepare a dough. Our instructions were: Combine 1 cup of water with 1 cup flour and knead until a smooth dough is formed.
- Roll the dough into 5 equal-sized balls and flatten each with a tortilla press (also available in the Spanish or Latin American shop) or between two inverted pots and two layers of cling film to form a flat cake with a diameter of about 10 cm.

- Heat a pan and bake the tortillas one by one. Bake it on one side until it starts to bulge in some places, then it's time to turn it over and let the other side tan a little.
- In the meantime, free the peppers from the core, cut them into fine stripes, finely slice the onions, crush the garlic, and roughly chop the coriander. Halve the zucchini, cut off the ends and cut into fine slices.
- Now heat the oil in the pan and first sauté the onion and the garlic, then add the peppers and the zucchini and simmer on a medium setting for about 10 minutes.
- After about 3 minutes add the tomato paste, mix everything well and then season with the spices, salt and pepper. As I said above, it's best to rely on your sense of taste and not so much on the information here, because everyone perceives the intensity of the spices differently.
- Now fill the tortillas with the filling, close them and sprinkle with coriander, lime and enjoy them directly. We tried them also when they were already cold – they were still delicious!

44. Thai Basil Corn Salad

Serving: Serves 8-10 | Prep: | Cook: |Ready in:

Ingredients

- 6-8 Ears of fresh sweet corn, shucked
- 1 Red bell pepper, diced small
- 10 ounces Cherry tomatoes
- 1/2 Red onion, finely diced
- 2 tablespoons Fresh lime juice
- 4 teaspoons Freshly ground black pepper
- 1 teaspoon Course kosher salt
- 4 teaspoons Garlic powder
- 4 tablespoons Extra virgin olive oil
- 1/2 cup Rice Wine Vinegar
- 1/4 cup Thai basil, finely chopped
- 1 teaspoon Sriracha or hot sauce (optional)

Direction

- Boil corn in lightly salted water for 8 minutes. Remove from water and let cool. When cool enough to handle cut kernels from cobs.
- Whisk together lime juice, olive oil, rice wine vinegar, pepper, salt and garlic powder.
- Toss together corn, red pepper, cherry tomatoes, red onion and Thai basil.
- Mix in dressing. Add Sriracha or hot sauce to taste. Cover with plastic wrap and refrigerate before serving at least 2 hours or overnight.

45. Tomato And Grilled Corn Salad With Smoked Salt

Serving: Serves 4 | Prep: | Cook: |Ready in:

Ingredients

- For the Salad
- 3 ears of corn
- 2 large heirloom tomatoes, about 1 pound total
- 1 pound smaller tomatoes, such as the zebra variety
- 4 ounces queso fresco
- 4 scallions, sliced thin
- 1 lime, zest only
- alderwood smoked salt
- For the vinaigrette
- 1 lime, juiced
- 1 pinch sea salt
- freshly ground pepper
- 1/2 cup extra-virgin olive oil

Direction

- Grill the Corn: Heat a grill to medium-high. Rub the ears of corn with a little olive oil and place them on the hot grill, covering with the lid. Cook the corn for about 10 minutes, turning every 2 minutes. You want some charring on the corn for flavor and color.

Remove the corn from the grill and set aside to cool while you prep the rest of the salad.
- Compose the Salad: Wash and dry the tomatoes. Cut the large tomatoes into big flat slices, horizontally (a serrated knife is best for cutting tomatoes). Cut the small tomatoes into wedges. I like a variety of textures and shapes in this salad. Place the tomato slices on a platter and artistically arrange the wedges. Take the cooled corn and cut it off the cob. Sprinkle the corn over the tomatoes on the platter. Crumble the queso fresco and arrange it over the tomatoes and corn. Toss scallions on top of the salad. Zest the lime over the salad.
- Make the Vinaigrette: Pour the lime juice with a sprinkling of regular salt and pepper into a small bowl. Drizzle in olive oil while whisking continuously to emulsify. Stop occasionally to taste the vinaigrette. Is it too acidic? Add more olive oil. Is the vinaigrette well balanced with lime and olive oil? Stop. It's finished! Drizzle the lime vinaigrette over the tomato and corn salad. Finish by sprinkling smoked salt over the salad. It's ready to serve.

46. Tuna And Corn Salad

Serving: Serves 4 | Prep: | Cook: |Ready in:

Ingredients

- 1 cup drained tuna
- 1 cup fresh mozzarella chopped (bite size pieces)
- 1 cup cooked sweet corn
- 20 cherry tomatoes (cut in half)
- 1 celery stalk chopped
- 1 green onion chopped
- 1/2 teaspoon salt
- 3-4 tablespoons olive oil
- 2 tablespoons balsamic vinegar
- 3-4 fresh basil leaves chopped
- 1 1/2 teaspoons oregano

Direction

- In a medium size bowl, add tuna, mozzarella, sweet corn, cherry tomatoes, celery, green onion, basil, oregano and toss gently, then in a small bowl mix salt and vinegar and pour over tuna mixture, then add the olive oil, gently toss together, let sit in fridge for 1 hour and serve. (If you prefer room temperature and your house isn't too hot, leave out for 1 hour before serving). Buon Appetito!

47. Warm Red Cabbage And Corn Salad

Serving: Serves 4 | Prep: | Cook: |Ready in:

Ingredients

- 2 ears of corn, corn kernels removed from the cob (or 1 1/2 cups frozen corn, thawed)
- 1/2 a head of a red cabbage, shredded very thin
- 2 tablespoons olive oil, divided
- 1 small red onion, thinly sliced
- 1 clove garlic, finely chopped
- 1/2 teaspoon smoked paprika
- 1/2 teaspoon salt
- pinch of cayenne pepper
- 2 tablespoons crumbled feta cheese
- 2 tablespoons pepitas, toasted
- 1 handful of chopped coriander/cilantro

Direction

- In a large pan heat 1 tablespoon olive oil over a medium high heat. Add corn kernels and season with salt and pepper. Cook, stirring frequently until slightly golden, about 5-8 minutes. Remove from pan and set aside.
- Heat remaining tablespoon of olive oil over a medium high heat. Add onion and cook for 2 minutes until softened. Add garlic and cook for another minute. Stir in paprika, salt and cayenne.

- Add cabbage and cook, stirring frequently, for about 2 minutes until the cabbage is just beginning to soften.
- Combine cabbage with corn and let cool for 5 minutes. Top with feta, pepitas and coriander and serve.

48. Anatomy Of A Grilled Corn Salad

Serving: Serves 4-6 | Prep: | Cook: | Ready in:

Ingredients

- 1 1/2 cups kernels cut off the grilled corn cob (4 small ears)
- 1/2 cup roasted edamame beans or lima beans (husked and oven roasted)
- 1-2 tablespoons grapeseed or olive oil for bean roasting
- 1/2-3/4 cups small red onion, chopped (a cipollini is great)
- 1-2 tablespoons chopped and seeded jalapeno pepper, to taste
- 1/2-1 teaspoons serrano or haberno pepper, chopped, optional
- 2 fresh limes, the juice of
- 1 teaspoon preferably pink salt (Himalayan or other type) to taste
- 1/2 cup fresh cilantro, bruised and chopped
- a handful of cherry heirloom tomatoes, sliced into halves, optional
- 1/8 cup basil, chopped, recommended
- 1/8 cup fresh spearmint, chopped, recommended
- 1/8 cup additional fresh chopped cilantro for second serving
- serving of Greek yogurt (fage) or sour cream on the side
- favorite tortilla chips for dipping if using salsa style
- additional medley of chopped cilantro, mint and basil for subsequent servings
- additional lime wedges to squeeze for subsequent servings

Direction

- Prepare your grill. I suggest hardwood coals with a handful of mesquite and alder wood chips.
- Trim off the raggle-taggle of your corn, including the stem a bit as well. Soak your corn in the husks in water; pull some of the husks down to expose the kernels of the cob so water can find its way to them. After soaking between 20 and 30 minutes, pull any husks back up to prepare for grilling.
- Grill your corn with the husks on. Depending upon your heat, this could take anywhere from 15 to 30 minutes. When the husks are dark brown, the corn should be cooked through, but check to see. If you want any caramelizing of your kernels, carefully turn down the husks for the last minute or two of grilling, taking care not to burn yourself in the process. Let your corn cool.
- Add the husked beans to a shallow dish with a small amount of grapeseed or olive oil. Roast for about 20- 30 minutes in a 350 degree oven until tender. Drain on paper towels and let cool.
- Combine with the chopped onions and hot peppers in a large bowl. Add the salt and let rest. Word of caution- do not handle the hot peppers directly. Use gloves or paper towels. Avoid that awful burn. If you handle them and then touch your eyes, nose, lips, you will have to suffer along...so wash your hands immediately with lots of soap in that event. Feel free to substitute sweet peppers. Add the cilantro. Pour the juice of two limes over this.
- Cut the corn off the cobs. Add 1 1/2 cups to the salad. Toss. Chill thoroughly and then serve. Add fresh garnish of a medley of herbs, chopped/chiffonade style with sour cream or fage on the side. Use also as a salsa and add your favorite chip.
- For a variation, add cherry heirloom tomatoes and basil. If you do not eat this all in one day,

it will keep nicely in the fridge for a few days. The flavors will bloom after chilling and settling. This holds up in the fridge well all week long, with the flavors improving each day. Just add additional fresh herbs on top each time you serve this along with a fresh squeeze of lime to reinvigorate.

49. Cake

Serving: Serves 28 | Prep: 10017hours2mins | Cook: 12345hours23mins | Ready in:

Ingredients

- 234 ounces ketchup
- 2589 bunches mustard
- 3703 liters peanut butter
- 3456 pieces pickle
- 23456 gallons apple
- 234 handfuls anything
- 63 quarts pork

Direction

- Put ketchup in the bowl
- Put everything in any order you'd like then eat right away

50. Quinoa And Corn Salad

Serving: Serves 4 | Prep: | Cook: |Ready in:

Ingredients

- 1 cup quinoa, cooked according to the package's instructions
- 4 ears of corn, kernals removed
- 1-2 shallots, finely minced
- 4 tablespoons olive oil
- 1/4 cup chopped parsley
- 1 tablespoon balsamic vinegar
- salt and pepper

Direction

- While you are cooking the quinoa, put 2 tablespoons of the olive oil in a pan over medium high heat and add the corn. Add salt and pepper to taste and cook for about 3-4 minutes.
- When all the water has been absorbed by the quinoa, uncover the pot and stir in the shallots. Cover and let stand for about five minutes.
- Stir in the cooked corn and the parsley, along with the remaining oil and the vinegar. Check the seasoning and serve.

Index

A
Avocado 3,8,11,13,17,23

B
Basil 3,18,24
Beans 15
Blackberry 3,9
Butter 3,10

C
Cabbage 3,25
Cake 3,27
Caramel 3,7
Cayenne pepper 14
Champ 5,20
Cheese 15
Cherry 12,23,24
Chilli 14
Chipotle 11
Cider 5
Cream 3,9,11
Crumble 5,25
Cucumber 15,17,18
Cumin 5,14

D
Dill 3,10

E
Edam 3,18

F
Feta 3,8,10,15,17
Fish 7

G
Garlic 5,14,18,24
Grain 3,22

H
Herbs 3,17
Honey 12,16

J
Jus 27

L
Lemon 15
Lime 3,5,7,11,13,17,18,20,23

M
Mayonnaise 11
Milk 22
Mint 3,16
Mustard 12

N
Nut 14

O
Oil 9,12,13,17
Olive 5,12,13,15,16,17
Onion 3,5,7,11,12,13,17,18
Oregano 15,18

P
Parsley 13
Pasta 3,4
Peel 18,21
Pepper 3,4,5,12,13,14,15,16,17,18
Pistachio 3,8
Potato 3,19,20

Q

Quinoa 3,8,27

R

Radicchio 3,8

Red onion 23,24

Rhubarb 3,18

Rice 12,24

Rosemary 3,5

S

Salad 1,3,4,5,6,7,8,9,10,11,12,13,14,15,16,17,18,19,20,21,22,23,24,25,26,27

Salmon 3,9

Salt 3,4,5,10,12,13,15,17,23,24

Seasoning 18,19

Shallot 3,8

Sherry 8

Soup 3,11

Sugar 5

T

Taco 3,6

Taro 8

Thai basil 24

Tomato 3,8,11,12,13,17,18,24

V

Vinegar 3,5,8,12,18,24

W

Walnut 15

Wine 12,18,24

Z

Zest 3,13,15,25

Conclusion

Thank you again for downloading this book!

I hope you enjoyed reading about my book!

If you enjoyed this book, please take the time to share your thoughts and post a review on Amazon. It'd be greatly appreciated!

Write me an honest review about the book – I truly value your opinion and thoughts and I will incorporate them into my next book, which is already underway.

Thank you!

If you have any questions, **feel free to contact at:** *author@slushierecipes.com*

Megan Murphy

slushierecipes.com

Made in the USA
Columbia, SC
17 November 2024

46730375R00017